GOLD LEAF BOOKS

Thanks are due for the expertise and knowledge of
Matthew Stevens of M Stevens & Son, fishmongers of St Ives

First edition published 2010, 2015
Second edition 2018
This edition 2021

ISBN 978 0 85025 480 8

Published by Tor Mark Ltd,
United Downs Industrial Estate,
St Day, Redruth, Cornwall TR16 5HY

www.tormark.co.uk

Printed and bound in the UK

CORNISH
FISH
RECIPES

Heather Corbett

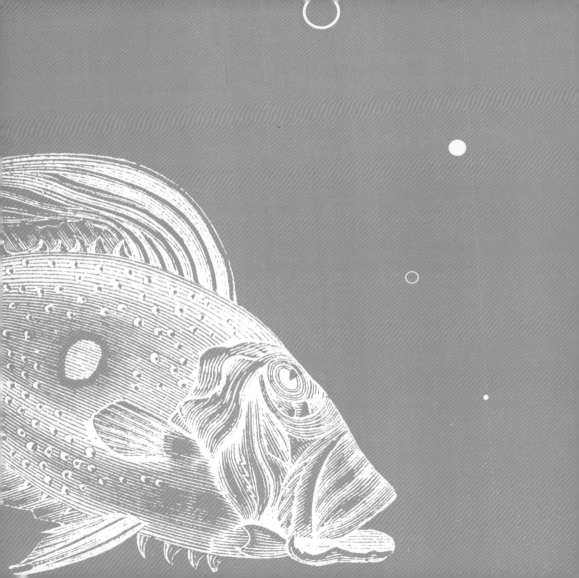

CONTENTS

AN INTRODUCTION

Fish is the original fast food – in earlier times, cooked quickly over a fire or baked in the embers. Fish is good for you! It does not have the calories of meat, yet it has a similar vitamin content. Oily fish like mackerel, herring and sardines have the added bonus of reducing the possibility of heart disease and strokes.

These recipes are easy, fast, successful and interesting. I have cooked – and adapted them – over the years for family and friends. Fish cookery is far more enticing and exciting than it used to be. Forget those childhood memories of fishy smells and a mouthful of bones – fish cooking has grown up and is the ultimate quality food in this busy world. Many of the recipes in this book are interchangeable – if you haven't got all the ingredients, be confident, substitute. Above all, be inventive and enjoy the results! Nearly all these recipes are cooked in a hot oven, giving a double advantage – the lack of smell and the fish is cooked very fast in one dish. Once it's in the oven you just have time for a sip of wine and voilà, your dinner is ready!

The fish used in these recipes are those caught all around the coast of the South West and sold at the fish markets of Newlyn, Padstow, Looe, Plymouth and Brixham. Much from these markets goes 'up country' or, sadly, is exported to Europe – Spain and France buy a good deal of British fish and in both countries, restaurants around the coast have a reputation for cooking 'local' fish! Newlyn has the second largest fishing fleet in Britain. You can walk along the quay, look at the fishing boats and see the fish market. Most of the boats are beam trawlers. They have a crew of five and fish up to 100 miles out, for a week at a time, in winds often reaching gale force before returning home for a few days.

Fish caught in the West Country are available throughout Britain in local fishmongers and at supermarket fish stalls. Whenever possible buy fish that is fresh, rather than frozen, and cook it quickly – that way the fish will have the best possible taste. Shop with an open mind – go for what looks good on the day.

Heather Corbett

BRILL WITH COURGETTES & WHITE WINE

Serves 4

Brill is a beautiful fish, so buy it when you see it. Sometimes they can be quite large and you may only need half a fillet per person. It is slightly thicker than lemon sole so takes a little longer to cook. The flesh is quite firm and delicately flavoured.

INGREDIENTS

4 brill fillets, trimmed

4 medium courgettes, finely sliced

200ml white wine

olive oil

For the sauce:

2 garlic cloves, finely chopped

6 tbsp Greek yoghurt

2 tbsp lemon juice

1 tbsp chives, chopped

4 cherry tomatoes, cut into quarters

Heat the oven to 200°C/390°F/gas mark 6. Place the fillets in an oiled ovenproof dish. Place the courgettes around the fish, add the white wine and a little more oil. Bake for 10-15 minutes. In the meantime, make the sauce by stirring all the ingredients together.

Serve the brill with the sauce on the side.

COD WITH CORIANDER & SAFFRON

Serves 4

This is an unusual use of cod, which makes a change from many other recipes, and is a very pretty dish. When cod is not available this dish would work well with silver mullet or pollack.

INGREDIENTS

4 150g pieces of cod fillet

1 tsp green peppercorns, crushed

1 tsp coriander seeds, crushed

12 strands of saffron

225ml white wine

110ml olive oil

12 cherry tomatoes

1 tbsp parsley, chopped

1 tbsp balsamic vinegar

Bring the white wine to the boil and pour over the roughly chopped green peppercorns, coriander seeds and saffron. Pour a little of the olive oil into an ovenproof dish, lay in the 4 pieces of cod and the cherry tomatoes. Cover with the saffron and white wine mix, and add a little more olive oil.

Cook in a hot oven 230ºC/450ºF/gas mark 8 for about 15 minutes. Before serving, add the balsamic vinegar and the parsley. Plain rice or couscous go well with this recipe.

COD WITH RUNNER BEANS

Serves 4

This is a surprising and wonderful dish based on a Jamie Oliver recipe that I found in a newspaper. The runner beans could be replaced by French beans.

INGREDIENTS

4 110-175g pieces of cod fillet

4 slices smoked bacon

450g runner beans, thinly sliced

12 cherry tomatoes

12 black olives

olive oil

2 lemons, halved

1 tbsp parsley or chives, chopped

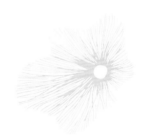

Place the beans, cherry tomatoes, lemons and olives in a lightly oiled ovenproof dish. Wrap the slices of bacon around each piece of cod, place amongst the beans and then drizzle with a little olive oil.

Cook in a hot oven 230ºC/450ºF/gas mark 8 for about 15 minutes, depending on the size of the cod. Decorate with the chopped parsley or chives. This dish goes well with plain rice or couscous.

COD WITH CUCUMBER, SPRING ONIONS & CREAM

Serves 4

Cooked cucumber may seem odd but it adds a wonderful colour and texture to the dish. Cod is more readily available than it used to be; I'm told that there are always plenty two miles off Newlyn in the spring.

INGREDIENTS

450g cod fillets, cut into large pieces

4 spring onions, finely chopped

10cm cucumber, roughly chopped

olive oil

1 glass white wine

200ml double cream

1 tsp dill or parsley, chopped

Drizzle a little olive oil onto the base of an ovenproof dish and add the cod fillets. Place the spring onions and cucumber on top of the fish and then add the white wine.

Bake in a hot oven 230°C/450°F/gas mark 8 for about 15 minutes, depending on the thickness of the fish. Add the cream and the dill or parsley, and return to the oven to heat through. This dish is good with new potatoes and French beans.

CRAB LINGUINE

Serves 4

This dish has become very popular in recent years as crabmeat has been more readily available in supermarkets. It is unbelievably easy to make. I think that linguine is essential for this dish. You can use other, more robust pasta, but it never seems the same to me as its texture becomes too dominant.

INGREDIENTS

300g linguine

3 small courgettes

olive oil

2 cloves garlic, chopped

pinch of chilli flakes

250g white crabmeat

50g brown crabmeat, if you can get it

6 spring onions, chopped

1 tbsp parsley chopped

Cook the linguine according to the packet instructions and drain. Meanwhile quickly fry the courgettes in some olive oil. Add the chopped garlic and a pinch of chilli flakes. Then mix with the linguine in a serving dish, add the crabmeat, spring onions and parsley and mix a little more to distribute the crab fully. Add a little olive oil to taste and serve.

FISHCAKES

Serves 4

Fishcakes are a wonderful way of using up leftover fish and potatoes. The most important thing to remember is getting the proportions right — one third potato to two thirds fish, but don't worry too much about the actual amounts.

Any kind of leftover fish can be used; salmon, cod, haddock, sole, plaice and crab all make excellent fishcakes. If you don't have quite enough fish, you can add a few roughly chopped prawns into the mix. I have even made fishcakes using tinned sardines with tomato! Of course, the fish does not have to be leftover if you are as fond of fishcakes as I am!

INGREDIENTS

450g leftover (cooked) fish

300g cooked potato, either mashed or roughly chopped

2 spring onions, finely chopped

pinch of chilli flakes

2 eggs, lightly beaten

1 tbsp parsley, chopped

For cooking & serving:

100g breadcrumbs (Panko are good)

olive or vegetable oil

2 lemons, cut into quarters

salad, for serving

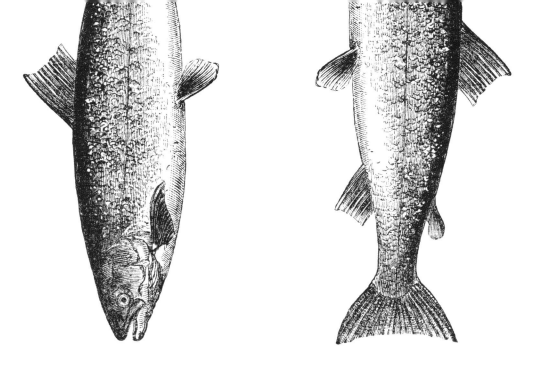

Gently mix all the above ingredients together. Shape into four rounds, approx 3cm across and 2cm thick. The fishcakes may be rather moist but don't worry. Add the breadcrumbs (Panko are good) to a plate and roll the cakes onto them, gently turning over so that both sides are covered. Cover and chill the cakes in the fridge for 2 hours to firm up.

Prepare a good-sized frying pan with sufficient oil to cook the cakes but without overwhelming them. Heat to a good temperature and place all the cakes in neatly. Cook so that they are brown on one side before carefully turning over with a fish slice – a lightness of touch is important if you don't want them to break up. They won't take long – remember that the ingredients are already cooked so all you are doing is cooking the outside coating and heating them through. Serve with quarters of lemon and a colourful salad.

FISH CRUMBLE

Serves 4

Any fish will do for this homely dish, although it's nice to get a range of textures – a little cooked salmon adds a lovely colour as well as texture and flavour.

INGREDIENTS

450g assorted white fish (see above)

20 cooked prawns (defrosted if using frozen)

2 hard boiled eggs, roughly chopped

1 tbsp parsley, chopped

4 spring onions, chopped

For the crumble:

40g butter

75g plain flour

50g Cheddar cheese, grated

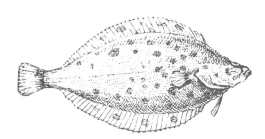

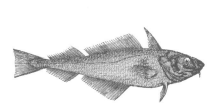

For the sauce:

40g butter

40g plain flour

250ml milk

125ml cider or white wine

Cornish sea salt and ground black pepper, to taste

Make the crumble by rubbing the butter into the flour to form breadcrumbs and then adding the cheese. Make the sauce, by melting the butter in a saucepan before mixing in the flour and allowing the two to cook for a moment. Add the milk and the cider or wine very slowly – being too enthusiastic here will cause the sauce to go lumpy. Season with salt and pepper to taste.

Place all the fish, prawns, egg, parsley and spring onions into an ovenproof dish and pour the sauce over. Top with the crumble mix and cook in a hot oven 230°C/450°F/gas mark 8 for 15-20 minutes until cooked through.

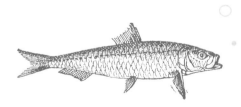

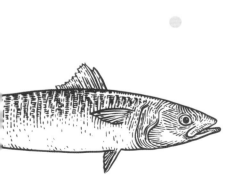

RED GURNARD FILLETS WITH CELERY & APPLE

Serves 4

Gurnard needs to be well filleted, as small pinbones left in can be very irksome. It has a good flavour and is quite firm. The skin is a beautiful pinky red which looks very pretty peeping through the sauce. It is available all the year round.

INGREDIENTS

4 red gurnard, filleted

3 sticks of celery, sliced thinly

2 apples, chopped into small chunks

4 spring onions, chopped

25g butter

275ml single cream

1 tbsp French flat leaf parsley, chopped

1 tbsp walnuts for decoration, chopped

broccoli and mashed potato, for serving

Butter an ovenproof dish. Place the gurnard fillets in it, and sprinkle the celery, apple and spring onions on top. Pour over the single cream, cover with tin foil and put in a hot oven 230°C/450°F/gas mark 8.

Cook for 10 minutes, uncover and cook for a further 5 minutes. Decorate with the parsley and the walnuts. Serve with broccoli and mashed potatoes sprinkled with some more French parsley.

GREEK HADDOCK

Serves 4

A dish that many will have had on holiday in the Mediterranean. Haddock or any other white fish can be used.

INGREDIENTS

4 150-175g pieces of haddock fillet

olive oil

1 glass white wine

1 lemon, squeezed

1 onion, chopped

2 cloves garlic, chopped

1 tbsp parsley, chopped

2 green peppers, chopped

4 large tomatoes, roughly chopped

4 medium potatoes, roughly sliced

Cornish sea salt and ground black pepper, to taste

Lightly oil an ovenproof dish. Place the potatoes in it and bake in the oven until lightly browned and nearly cooked. Fry the onion, garlic and peppers in olive oil until nearly soft, add the tomatoes, the lemon juice, wine, parsley, salt and pepper to taste and simmer for 5 minutes until nearly cooked.

Place the haddock fillets on top of the nearly cooked potatoes and cover with the vegetable mixture. Add a little more liquid if it seems dry. Cook for 20 minutes in a medium oven 180°C/350°F/gas mark 4 or until the fish is cooked.

HADDOCK WITH MUSHROOMS & COURGETTES

Serves 4

Haddock is much enhanced by the combination of mushrooms and courgettes. You can use pieces from a large fillet of haddock, or smaller whole fillets.

INGREDIENTS

4 125g pieces of haddock

150g chestnut mushrooms, sliced

2 medium courgettes, thinly sliced

2 tbsp capers

olive oil

125ml white wine

2 tbsp chives or spring onions, chopped

Heat the oven to 200°C/390°F/gas mark 6. Place the mushrooms and courgettes in an oiled ovenproof dish. Drizzle some olive oil over them and cook in the oven for 10 minutes. Remove from the oven and stir, then place the haddock fillets on top. Sprinkle with the capers, a little olive oil and the white wine. Cook for 8 minutes, unless the haddock is very thick – in which case it will take a little longer.

Remove from the oven and serve decorated with the chives or spring onions.

SMOKED HADDOCK & MUSHROOM LASAGNE

Serves 4

Surprisingly, fish makes a good lasagne – shellfish can also be used successfully.

INGREDIENTS

450g smoked haddock fillets, cooked and flaked

1 onion, roughly chopped

110g mushrooms, chopped

1 400g tin chopped tomatoes

paprika

Cornish sea salt and ground black pepper, to taste

1 tbsp parsley, chopped

olive oil

9 sheets egg lasagne – the sort that does not require pre-cooking

275ml plain yoghurt

1 egg

4 tbsp Parmesan, grated

Fry the onion and the mushrooms in a little oil to soften. Add the tomatoes, a large pinch of paprika, sea salt and ground black pepper, to taste. Cook for 5 minutes.

In an oiled ovenproof dish, place a third of the smoked haddock, then a third of the tomato sauce mixture. Place 3 sheets of lasagne on top. Repeat twice more.

Mix the yoghurt, egg and 3 tablespoons Parmesan together and spread over the last layer of lasagne. Sprinkle the remaining Parmesan on top.

Bake in a medium oven 180°C/350°F/gas mark 4 for 25 minutes or until cooked. Decorate with parsley.

SMOKED HADDOCK & SPINACH TART

Serves 4

Smoked fish and spinach seem to be natural companions and in a tart, the mix of colours is delightful.

INGREDIENTS

For the pastry:

110g plain flour

50g butter

water to mix

For the filling:

450g spinach cooked, well drained and chopped

225g smoked haddock, cooked and flaked

2 tomatoes

3 eggs

275ml milk

150ml double cream

1 tbsp Parmesan, grated

1 tbsp parsley, chopped

Cornish sea salt and ground black pepper, to taste

Make the pastry in the usual way, rubbing the butter into the flour and adding the water to mix – place in the fridge to keep cool. Whisk the eggs with the milk, cream and the parsley, and season to taste with coarse sea salt and ground black pepper.

Roll out the pastry and place in a 20cm flan dish. Add the spinach and the haddock, and pour over the egg mix to cover. Slice the tomatoes and arrange decoratively on top, and sprinkle with Parmesan. Bake at 180°C/350°F/gas mark 4 for 35-40 minutes until cooked.

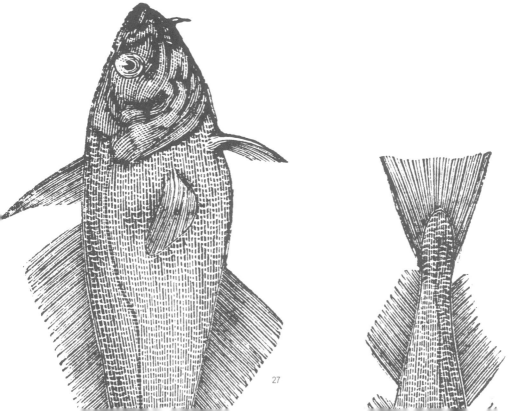

SPANISH HAKE

Serves 4

Much of the hake caught in our waters is exported to Spain, where it is highly valued. If you are lucky enough to find some hake in your fishmonger's, do not hesitate to buy it — it has enough character to be combined with strong Mediterranean flavours. This recipe is based on one found in Spain on holiday. It was so good, I had to bring it home!

INGREDIENTS

4 110g pieces of hake

50g chorizo sausage, chopped into small cubes

1 large onion, chopped

2 medium courgettes, sliced thinly

1 400g tin chopped tomatoes

olive oil

150ml sherry

¼ tsp paprika

1 lemon, sliced into wedges

Cornish sea salt and ground black pepper, to taste

plain boiled rice and lemon wedges, for serving

First, fry the chopped onion and the chorizo together. When softened, place in the bottom of an ovenproof dish. Add the 4 pieces of hake, and cover them with the thin slices of courgette and the paprika. Mix the chopped tomatoes and the sherry, add a little salt and pepper, and pour over the assembled ingredients.

Place in a hot oven 230°C/450°F/gas mark 8 for 20 minutes, depending on the thickness of the hake. Serve with plain boiled rice and lemon wedges.

HAKE WITH HERB & CAPER SAUCE

Serves 4

This recipe for hake uses ingredients which are a change from those usually inspired by the Mediterranean. Hake is a robust fish but it can be rather dry, which this sauce helps to soften.

INGREDIENTS

4 125g pieces of hake

125ml white wine

olive oil

4 spring onions, chopped

black pepper

For the sauce:

100ml mayonnaise

100g Greek yoghurt

2 tbsp lemon juice

2 tsp capers

2 tbsp mixed herbs – chives, parsley, mint, chopped

Heat the oven to 200°C/390°F/gas mark 6. Place the hake pieces in an oiled ovenproof dish. Drizzle a little white wine and olive oil over them, along with the chopped spring onions and a little black pepper. Bake in the oven for 10 minutes. Using a sharp knife, gently check the fish is cooked – it should look firm and fresh – not watery. Depending on thickness it may need a further 5 minutes.

To make the sauce mix the mayonnaise, yogurt, lemon juice, capers and herbs together. Depending on your preference, you can either pour the sauce over the cooked fish or serve it separately. New potatoes go very well with this dish.

HAKE STEAKS WITH LEMON & GREEN OLIVES

Serves 4

If hake is difficult to find, then cod is a good substitute.

INGREDIENTS

4 110g hake steaks

juice of 1 lemon

2 tbsp olive oil and a little more

1 tbsp parsley, chopped

2 cloves garlic, chopped

4 tbsp breadcrumbs

Cornish sea salt and ground black pepper, to taste

12 green olives, pitted and roughly chopped

First, marinate the hake steaks in the lemon juice and olive oil for at least an hour – or longer if possible. Mix together the breadcrumbs, parsley, salt, pepper and garlic.

Place the fish in an ovenproof dish with the marinade – sprinkle the breadcrumb topping over the fish and place in a hot oven 230°C/450°F/gas mark 8 for 20 minutes. Decorate with the olives before serving. Rice goes well with this dish.

RED FILLETS OF JOHN DORY

Serves 4

John Dory is an unusual fish with a good texture which flakes slightly when cut with a knife. It is firm, so the fillets hold their shape when cooked. It is available for much of the year.

INGREDIENTS

2 John Dory, filleted

16 cherry tomatoes

1 red pepper, thinly sliced

olive oil

juice of ½ a lemon

4 spring onions, finely chopped

1 tsp parsley, chopped

small pinch of paprika

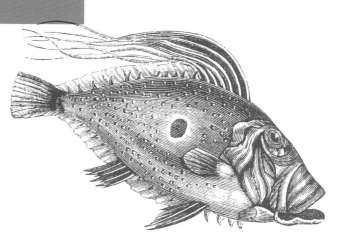

Pour a small quantity of olive oil in an ovenproof dish. Cut the fillets of John Dory in half lengthways and place on top.

Add the red pepper, cherry tomatoes, lemon juice and paprika, cover with tin foil and place in a hot oven 230ºC/450ºF/gas mark 8 for about 15 minutes. Uncover and add the spring onions and parsley.

This is very good served with a small quantity of mushroom and herb risotto.

PEPPERED HERRING

Serves 4

Herring is around for much of the year, is readily available and is reasonably versatile. It has quite a strong flavour and a creamy texture. One of the most successful recipes is herring dipped in oatmeal — here is an interesting variation.

INGREDIENTS

4 herrings, filleted

olive oil

1 tbsp black peppercorns

1 tbsp flour

dash of balsamic vinegar (if liked)

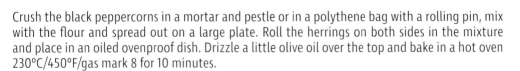

Crush the black peppercorns in a mortar and pestle or in a polythene bag with a rolling pin, mix with the flour and spread out on a large plate. Roll the herrings on both sides in the mixture and place in an oiled ovenproof dish. Drizzle a little olive oil over the top and bake in a hot oven 230°C/450°F/gas mark 8 for 10 minutes.

Serve with a dash of balsamic vinegar on top. A robust red wine, French bread and French beans are excellent with this dish.

RED MULLET WITH PASTA,
CHERRY TOMATOES, BLACK OLIVES & HERBS

Serves 4

Red mullet is such a pretty fish because of its pinky red skin, but other fish could be used, for example, haddock, gurnard or even sea bass. Choose whatever pasta you have to hand — spaghetti, farfalle or orecchiette.

INGREDIENTS

300g pasta of your choice

4 250g mullet fillets

16 cherry tomatoes, halved

24 black olives, stoned

2 garlic cloves, peeled and chopped

olive oil

pinch chilli flakes, to taste

1 lemon, cut into quarters

2 handfuls basil, torn

Heat the oven to 200°C/390°F/gas mark 6. Cook the pasta until al dente. Place the halved tomatoes, olives and garlic in a small roasting tin and cook in a little oil for 5 minutes. Place the mullet fillets on top and sprinkle with chilli to taste. Cook for a further 7 minutes, depending on the thickness of the fish.

Drain the pasta into a serving dish and then add the tomatoes and mullet fillets, breaking up the fish as you go. Serve with a drizzle of olive oil, the lemon quarters and 2 handfuls of torn basil.

SILVER MULLET
WITH ROASTED VEGETABLES

Serves 4

Although the name silver mullet does not sound very enticing, it is a fine fish – quite firm and robust. They can be a good size, one fish between two may be plenty!

INGREDIENTS

2 silver mullet, filleted

1 red pepper, cut into chunks

2 medium courgettes, roughly chopped

2 small red onions, roughly chopped

2 sprigs of thyme

1 ripe avocado, chopped into small cubes

275ml natural yoghurt

¼ tsp paprika

3 tbsp olive oil

Cornish sea salt and ground black pepper, to taste

Place the vegetables in an ovenproof dish with 2 tablespoons of the olive oil. Add the sprigs of thyme and a little salt and pepper. Roast in a hot oven 230°C/450°F/gas mark 8 for 20 minutes. Remove from the oven; place the silver mullet fillets on top, flesh side up. Drizzle the remainder of the olive oil over the fish and return to the oven for a further 10 minutes, or until the fish is cooked.

While the fish is cooking, make the avocado raita by combining the yoghurt and the chopped avocado. Sprinkle a little paprika on the top as decoration. This raita should be offered with the fish, rather than being poured over it. New potatoes go well with this dish.

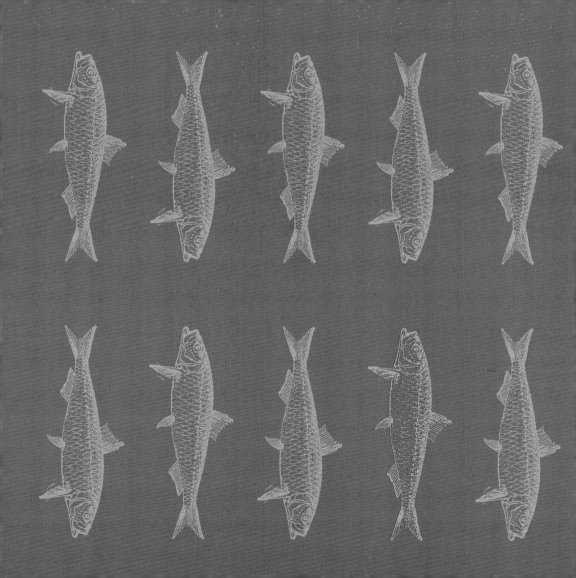

MARINADES FOR MACKEREL OR SARDINES

Serves 4

Mackerel and Sardines barbeque particularly well and are so easy to prepare. The natural oil in the fish keeps them succulent. These marinades provide a delicate taste without detracting from the natural fish flavours.

INGREDIENTS

For these recipes, use 4 mackerel or at least 8 sardines depending on the size.

Lemon & ginger marinade:

2 tbsp olive oil

3 tbsp soy sauce

1 clove garlic, finely grated

2 tbsp lemon juice

1 tbsp fresh ginger*, finely grated

*or lemon zest

Mediterranean marinade:

2 tbsp olive oil

1 tbsp red or white wine vinegar

1 tbsp tomato puree

1 tbsp capers

1 tsp dried oregano

ground black pepper, to taste

Pesto marinade:

2 tbsp olive oil

2 tbsp pesto

2 tsp balsamic vinegar

First, choose your marinade! Place all the ingredients for the marinade in a dish and whisk together vigorously. Allow to stand while you prepare your fish by washing thoroughly under cold water and laying on kitchen paper. Pat gently all over to dry. Now, simply add your fish to your marinade and swirl around gently. I like to use a silicone pastry brush to make sure every part of the fish is coated in the glorious marinade.

Cover and leave to rest for at least an hour, or as long as you can.

Once the BBQ is ready, place the fish on, preferably with a medium heat below. Turn gently but frequently as they cook, basting regularly with the remaining marinade left in the bowl. Mackerel and sardines cook very quickly. To check that they are cooked, gently prise apart the flesh underneath the fish; it should be firm but not watery.

BAKED MACKEREL
WITH CIDER, ORANGE & CHIVES

Serves 4

Fresh mackerel is a beautiful fish to look at – silver and blue green. It is essential that it's eaten as fresh as possible – it does not keep well; this is why so much is smoked (the best mackerel for smoking are those caught during the winter months from November to March, as they are much more oily). Increasingly mackerel in the South West is line caught – these are the ones you should buy to ensure that mackerel fishing is sustainable. The orange in this recipe offsets the oiliness of the fish.

INGREDIENTS

4 mackerel fillets

150ml cider

2 oranges

4 spring onions, chopped

olive oil

Cornish sea salt and ground black pepper, to taste

Grate the orange rind, peel the oranges and cut into slices. Place half the orange slices on the base of an ovenproof dish, arrange the mackerel fillets on top, place the remainder of the orange slices over the fish and then sprinkle the orange rind and the spring onions on top. Pour the cider over the fish and season with sea salt and ground black pepper.

Place in a hot oven 230ºC/450ºF/gas mark 8 for 10-15 minutes until cooked. Serve with French bread and a salad, which are excellent with this dish.

SMOKED MACKEREL INSTANT PASTA

Serves 4

In Cornwall and Devon there are a number of small firms smoking not only mackerel, haddock and cod but all sorts of fish and meats. Smoked mackerel adds a distinctive flavour to old favourites, such as cauliflower or macaroni cheese. Simply flake the smoked mackerel fillets and add to the cheese sauce.

INGREDIENTS

4 smoked mackerel fillets, flaked

450g fresh pasta

570ml single cream

1 tbsp Parmesan, grated

4 spring onions, roughly chopped

225g mushrooms, roughly chopped

butter

Cornish sea salt and ground black pepper, to taste

1 tbsp parsley, chopped

Gently cook the mushrooms and spring onions in the melted butter, in a saucepan, for 5 minutes over a medium heat until softened. Add the flaked, smoked mackerel and heat through, and then add the cream, making sure that you do not allow it to boil.

Cook the fresh pasta as directed on the packet, place in a serving dish, add the mackerel, mushrooms, spring onions and the grated Parmesan, and mix together lightly. Sprinkle with the chopped parsley and ground black pepper to taste.

SMOKED MACKEREL, POTATOES & LEEKS

Serves 4

Smoked mackerel is a useful store cupboard fish, as it keeps for some time vacuum-packed in the fridge or even longer in the freezer. This is a truly classic dish and can be prepared in a number of ways very effectively.

INGREDIENTS

4 small smoked mackerel fillets

2 medium leeks, cut across into 5mm slices

275ml single cream

200ml milk

1 tbsp grain mustard or horseradish sauce

450g potatoes, peeled and cut into 5mm slices

butter

Cornish sea salt and ground black pepper, to taste

Butter an ovenproof dish. Place in it a layer of potatoes, then leeks, then the flaked, smoked mackerel. Repeat this and finish with a layer of potato.

Mix together the cream, milk and mustard or horseradish. Carefully pour this over the top so that it goes through the layers, adding ground black pepper to taste. Cover with tin foil and put in a hot oven 230°C/450°F/gas mark 8 for about 50 minutes.

Test the middle of the dish with a skewer to see if the potato is cooked — when this is the case, remove the tin foil and cook for another 10 minutes to brown the potatoes on top.

STUFFED SARDINES

Serves 4

Sardines are such a versatile fish, full of flavour. They are caught in the South West during the summer when they are plentiful and cheap. Once de-headed, gutted and de-boned, but still remaining in one piece, they lend themselves very well to stuffing. Almost anything will taste good — be inventive!

INGREDIENTS

12 sardines, de-boned

For mushroom stuffing:

6 salted sardine fillets or anchovies, roughly chopped

110g mushrooms, roughly chopped

1 small onion, roughly chopped

1 tsp dried oregano

1 tbsp tomato purée

olive oil

ground black pepper, to taste

For red pepper stuffing:

1 small red onion, roughly chopped

1 red pepper, roughly chopped

1 tbsp pine nuts

1 tbsp sultanas

1 tbsp tomato purée

1 tbsp French parsley, roughly chopped

olive oil

ground black pepper, to taste

Fry the onion and the mushrooms in a little olive oil until softened. Add the remainder of the ingredients and mix well before stuffing the sardines. Place in an ovenproof dish and bake in a hot oven 230°C/450°F/gas mark 8 for 10 minutes. Serve with lemon quarters and salad. For red pepper stuffing, cook and serve in the same way.

SARDINES WITH MUSTARD & CIDER

Serves 4

Sardines are in fact young pilchards and are caught off the Devon and Cornwall coasts in late summer. It is wonderful to see such shiny fresh fish. Sardines, as we prefer to call them (pilchards for us are tinned in tomato sauce), hardly need any preparation at all, simply gutting. If you can't cope with the bones, buy them de-boned but remaining in one piece. You may also find them ready prepared in your local supermarket. They are excellent simply grilled on the barbecue, but they can also be cooked in more exotic ways.

INGREDIENTS

12 sardines, de-boned

3 tbsp coarse grain mustard

olive oil

225ml cider

new potatoes, for serving

1 medium courgette, roughly chopped, or spinach, for serving

Place the sardines in an oiled ovenproof dish.

Smear each one outside and inside with the mustard and then pour enough cider into the dish to come halfway up the sardines. Bake in a hot oven 230°C/450°F/gas mark 8 for 10 minutes. You may need to top up the cider halfway through the cooking time.

Serve with new potatoes and a green vegetable such as courgettes or spinach.

SUMMER FISH WITH BRIE

Serves 4

This is a very useful way of using up any leftover cooked white fish — cod, pollack, silver mullet, monkfish, plaice, sole ... anything will be fine. This recipe is so good it is worth cooking fish especially for it — simply poach the fish in a little white wine and then leave to cool. I only poach fish in the summer when I can leave the windows and doors open, hence the name!

INGREDIENTS

450g cooked white fish

a little white wine

175g mushrooms, thinly sliced

2 cloves of garlic, crushed

2 tbsp chives and/or parsley, chopped

ground black pepper

225g Brie, cut into 6mm slices, rind left on

butter

Flake the cooked fish into bite-sized chunks. Butter an ovenproof serving dish and place the fish in one layer. The finely sliced mushrooms are placed on top of this with a little ground black pepper, 1 tablespoon of the herbs and the crushed garlic. Finally add a layer of Brie.

Place in a hot oven 230°C/450°F/gas mark 8 for 15 minutes when the Brie should be wonderfully runny. Decorate with the remainder of the chopped herbs. New potatoes and peas or French beans go beautifully with this dish.

MONKFISH RISOTTO WITH SAFFRON

Serves 4

Monkfish, tuna, shellfish and squid all lend themselves to being made into risotto.

INGREDIENTS

450g monkfish fillet, cut into bite-size chunks

1 onion, chopped

2 green peppers, chopped

2 cloves garlic, crushed

12 saffron threads

½ tsp paprika

225g Arborio risotto rice

1 glass white wine, vermouth or sherry

425ml fish or vegetable stock

1 tbsp French parsley, chopped

a few (defrosted) cooked prawns, for decoration

1 lemon, cut into wedges

Cornish sea salt and ground black pepper, to taste

olive oil

Fry the monkfish pieces in oil in a large frying or paella pan until they are nearly cooked. Remove and set aside. Fry the onion, garlic and the peppers gently until soft, then add the rice, stirring so that all the grains are covered with oil. Cover with the hot stock in which you have infused the saffron, and add the wine, vermouth or sherry, paprika, salt and pepper. Leave on a medium heat to cook – do not stir.

After 10 minutes return the monkfish to the pan, pushing it into and amongst the rice. Continue to simmer until the rice is cooked and the liquid has more or less evaporated. If the rice is not cooked but is dry, add a little more liquid – water or wine – and continue to cook.

Decorate with prawns, lemon wedges and parsley.

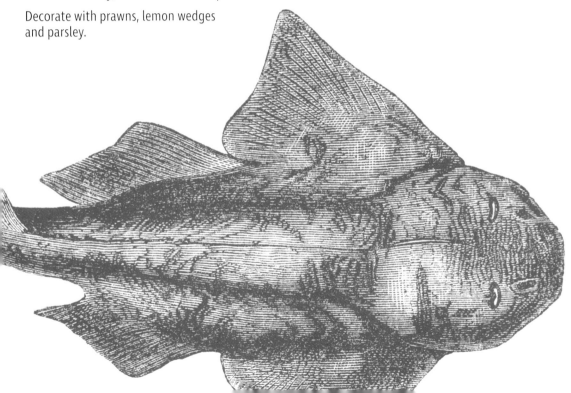

MONKFISH & BACON

Serves 4

This is a traditional French recipe which is always a surprise when brought to the table. Monkfish is a versatile fish, as it can be used in a number of ways — either in large pieces which are 'carved' as here, or in smaller pieces for a risotto. It is available all year round. The recipes for tuna stew (page 81) or squid with garlic, coriander and olives (page 76) would do very well with monkfish.

INGREDIENTS

700g monkfish tail in one piece

4-6 rashers of smoked bacon

8 sage leaves

2 cloves garlic, crushed

olive oil

balsamic vinegar or lemon juice

Firstly make sure that the fishmonger has taken the central bone out of the monkfish and cleaned off all the skin. The fish should still be more or less in one piece.

Arrange the sage leaves and the garlic along the length of the fish and then wrap the bacon rashers around it. Put in an oiled roasting pan and drizzle a little olive oil over it. Place in a hot oven 230°C/450°F/gas mark 8 for 30 minutes.

Remove the fish to a serving dish and drizzle a little balsamic vinegar or lemon juice over. The fish should be served in slices about 4cm thick. This dish would be very good with thickly cut sauté potatoes and a green salad.

MONKFISH, TOMATO & PEPPER KEBABS

Serves 4

Kebabs are good fun to make and serve. They are brightly coloured and look exciting to eat, especially when using a spicy marinade. They can be served with pitta bread, French baguette, couscous or rice.

INGREDIENTS

450g monkfish tail skinned with the backbone removed

2 large red peppers

20 cherry tomatoes

4 pitta breads/French baguette or 4 servings of cooked rice or couscous

For the marinade:

4 tbsp olive oil

1 tbsp lemon juice

1 tbsp sweet chilli sauce

1 tbsp chives or spring onions, chopped

Make the marinade by whisking all the ingredients together in a bowl. Cut the monkfish into 3cm cubes and place in the marinade for at least 1 hour.

Slice the peppers in half and remove the stalk and seeds before cutting them into suitable sized chunks for your skewers. Oil the skewers and thread them with the fish, pepper chunks and the cherry tomatoes. Baste the kebabs with some of the marinade. These can be made a few hours ahead – just pop them in the fridge if you aren't going to cook them immediately.

When you're ready to cook, place the kebabs on the BBQ and turn as they cook, basting as you go.

When they are beautifully browned and smelling wonderful, serve in a pitta bread or French baguette or accompanied by couscous or rice.

NOTE: tuna, salmon or large prawns would also be suitable for this recipe.

WEST COUNTRY PLAICE

Serves 4

Plaice is a succulent, delicate fish, so it is important not to overwhelm it with strong flavoured ingredients. The addition of cider and Cheddar cheese gives a West Country interest while the tomato adds colour. Plaice is at its best from May to December.

INGREDIENTS

4 plaice fillets

225g onion or leeks (which are prettier), chopped

2 tomatoes, thinly sliced

150ml dry cider

50g Cheddar cheese, grated

butter

1 tbsp dill, chopped

Cornish sea salt and ground black pepper, to taste

Fry the onion or leek in butter until softened and then put in an ovenproof dish. Add the four plaice fillets on top of the onion/leek, and put the sliced tomato on top. Sprinkle the cheese and most of the dill over the fish. Add sea salt and ground black pepper to taste, and drizzle the cider into the dish.

Place in a hot oven 230°C/450°F/gas mark 8 for about 10 minutes before serving. Decorate with the remaining dill.

PLAICE WITH GARLIC MUSHROOMS

Serves 4

Garlic mushrooms are a very popular starter. Here they make plaice into a luscious main course.

INGREDIENTS

4 small or 2 large plaice, filleted

4 cloves garlic, chopped

225g mushrooms, finely chopped

50g butter

1 tbsp parsley, finely chopped

150ml white wine

1 lemon, cut into curls or wedges

Cornish sea salt and ground black pepper, to taste

Soften the butter and beat into it the chopped garlic, parsley and mushrooms. If the plaice are large, cut the fillets in half lengthways. Pour a little of the white wine into an ovenproof dish, place half the fillets on top, spread the mushroom mixture over them and then place the other fillets on top, making a kind of sandwich. Add sea salt and ground black pepper to taste. Cover with the remainder of the wine.

Put in a hot oven 230°C/450°F/gas mark 8 for 15-20 minutes, depending on the thickness of the plaice – check after 15 minutes to be on the safe side. Decorate with the lemon, which takes away some of the richness of the buttery sauce.

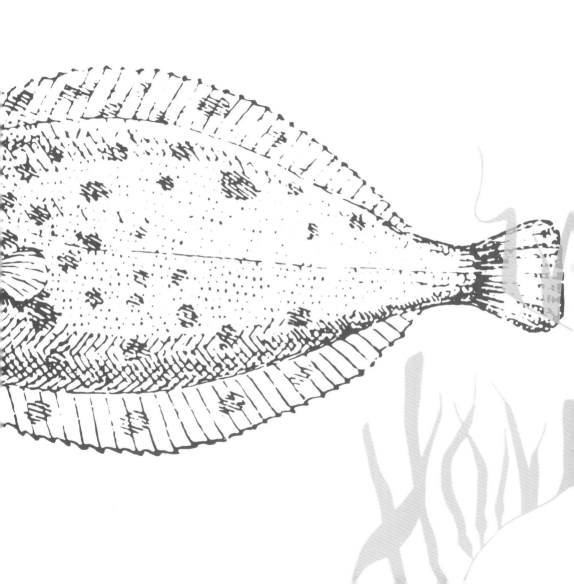

POLLACK WITH MAYONNAISE & YOGHURT

Serves 4

For years pollack has been ignored as a cheap fish and so much of it is exported to Brittany, but now that cod is expensive and less readily available it is coming into its own. The fillets are usually a good size and therefore can be cut into customised portions. It is best from August to March. Mayonnaise and yoghurt seems an odd combination but it makes a very satisfying sauce.

INGREDIENTS

4 portions of pollack fillet

4 spring onions, chopped

4 tbsp mayonnaise

4 tbsp plain yoghurt

4 tbsp breadcrumbs

butter

¼ tsp paprika

½ glass white wine, for marinade

First, marinate the fillets in the wine for 3-4 hours. Then place the fillets in a buttered ovenproof dish with the marinade, and cover with the mayonnaise and yoghurt, previously mixed together. Top with the breadcrumbs mixed with the chopped spring onions.

Place in a hot oven 230°C/450°F/gas mark 8 for 15 minutes and serve decorated with a sprinkling of paprika.

SCALLOP SALAD

Serves 4

Scallops are so delicious – 'little sweeties' as Rick Stein recently called them. In this recipe they are lovely surprises in the middle of a salad.

INGREDIENTS

16 scallops, cleaned and cut in half

2-4 tbsp olive oil

For the salad:

1 or 2 Little Gem lettuces (depending on size)

small handful of rocket leaves

12 cherry tomatoes, halved

cucumber chunks, as desired

8 radishes, halved

4 spring onions, chopped

12 black olives, stoned

1 tbsp capers

2 tbsp lemon Juice

1 tsp lemon zest

Cornish sea salt and black pepper, to taste

Start with the salad. Place all the ingredients together in a bowl, apart from the last 5 items (in *italics*) in the ingredients list. To cook the scallops, heat 2 tbsp of the olive oil before gently frying them over a medium heat. Turn each scallop gently and occasionally when the whiteness is firm and in no time at all, they will be cooked. Avoid overcooking them.

Once cooked, add the capers, lemon juice and zest. Be careful, the addition of the lemon juice will make the contents of the pan spit. You may need to add a little more olive oil. While still hot, add the scallops and dressing to the salad and toss carefully. Add a little salt and black pepper, to taste.

SCALLOPS WITH LEEKS & CORIANDER

Serves 4

Scallops are at their best from December to March. Although 24 scallops will be quite expensive, the superb flavour is not diluted by adding other tastes to pad it out, there is no waste and the dish is prepared and cooked in less than 10 minutes. Halve the ingredients to make an elegant starter.

INGREDIENTS

24 scallops, cleaned and cut in half

450g leeks, washed and cut into 6mm slices

juice of 1 lemon

1 tbsp coriander, chopped

olive oil

ground black pepper

fresh bread or new potatoes, for serving

Fry the leeks in the olive oil in a frying pan on a medium heat for 2-3 minutes, until beginning to soften. Add the scallops and fry until they start to colour and become soft. Add the lemon juice, ground black pepper and chopped coriander to the scallop juices, and heat through. Serve with fresh bread or new potatoes.

RED, WHITE & GREEN SCALLOPS

Serves 4

This is a wonderfully fresh and colourful dish and takes no time at all to cook and prepare. Asparagus makes it rather special, but another green vegetable such as fresh peas or French beans is just as good — perfect food for a summer's evening.

INGREDIENTS

24 scallops, cleaned and sliced in half

225g cherry tomatoes

1 large onion, roughly chopped

1 red pepper, finely chopped

225g chopped asparagus, peas or French beans, already lightly cooked

olive oil

1 glass white wine

2 tbsp coriander or parsley, chopped

Gently fry the onion and the red pepper, and when they are just beginning to soften and colour add the tomatoes. As the tomato skins begin to split, press each one to allow some of the juice to escape. Add the scallops and cook gently for a minute, before adding the wine and asparagus. Cook until the scallops are soft, gently stir through the coriander or parsley.

Rice, flavoured by cooking 2 quarters of a lemon in the water, is excellent with this dish.

SEA BASS PARCEL WITH VERMOUTH & LEEK

Serves 4

Barbeques are a quick and easy way to cook fish. Well-oiled fish-shaped grids can help to prevent larger fish from breaking up. Alternatively, making tin foil parcels is a brilliant way to barbeque almost any fish.

INGREDIENTS

4 sea bass fillets

2 leeks, finely chopped

pinch of dried chilli flakes, to taste

juice of 1 lemon and grated zest (kept separate)

150ml vermouth or dry white wine

olive oil

Light and prepare the BBQ.

Make 4 squares of doubled tin foil dull side out. Oil each square. Place 1 fillet of sea bass in each square. Sprinkle over the leeks and season with the chilli flakes and lemon zest. Fold the squares up, leaving a hole in the top. Pour the lemon juice, the vermouth or white wine and a little olive into a jug, whisk lightly with a fork before pouring a quarter of the liquid into each parcel. Seal the parcels well and carefully to keep your sauce inside!

Once the BBQ is ready, place the 4 parcels on the grid for about 4 minutes each side. Check to see if the fish is cooked (don't burn yourself!) When ready, split open each bag and serve. This recipe can also be baked in a 200°C/390°F/gas mark 6 oven for 15 minutes.

SEA BASS WITH FRESH HERB BUTTER

Serves 4

Much of the bass on sale is farmed; fresh wild sea bass is caught in the waters of the South West. It is at its best between June and February. Unfortunately, it is expensive, but it is worth buying once in a while, as it is a superb fish and best cooked simply.

INGREDIENTS

4 sea bass fillets

50g butter, softened

1 dessertspoon French parsley

1 dessertspoon chives

1 tsp thyme

½ glass white wine or dry sherry

olive oil

Cornish sea salt and ground black pepper, to taste

Mix the herbs with the softened butter. Place the sea bass fillets in an ovenproof dish and smear with the butter mixture. Season to taste and pour the wine or sherry around the fish.

Place in a hot oven 230°C/450°F/gas mark 8 for 10 minutes. Watch the cooking time carefully – the fish should only be just done and the butter not burnt.

Serve with some extravagant vegetable such as asparagus or really fresh garden peas. Nothing could be finer.

SEAFOOD WITH MUSTARD & CREAM

Serves 4

This recipe is in homage to Rick Stein, who has done so much to promote fish and fish cookery over the years. It is based on his seafood *thermidor*, an early recipe much loved by those who went to his restaurant – although made simpler for this book.

The original recipe is in *English Seafood Cookery* (Penguin, 1988) by 'Richard' Stein!

INGREDIENTS

450g assorted filleted white fish – it does not matter which fish, except that there needs to be a variety of textures

4 scallops, cleaned and cut in half

110g cooked shelled prawns

110g button mushrooms, halved

1 leek, thinly sliced

butter

½ glass white wine

juice of half a lemon

275ml double cream mixed with ½ tbsp English mustard powder

1 heaped tbsp Parmesan, grated

1 tbsp parsley, chopped

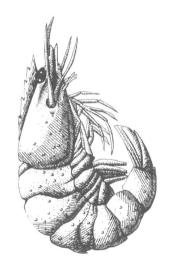

Place the leek, mushrooms, fish and scallops in a buttered ovenproof dish with the white wine and the lemon juice. Bake in a hot oven 230°C/450°F/gas mark 8 for 8 minutes and then drain off the liquid.

Add the prawns and then pour over the cream and the mustard mixture. Sprinkle the Parmesan across the top and return to the oven for a further 5 minutes, until the fish is cooked and the cream bubbling. Decorate with the parsley before serving. New potatoes and spinach are excellent with this dish.

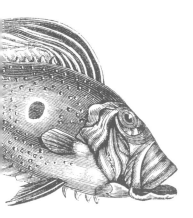

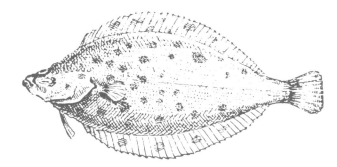

LEMON SOLE
WITH PRAWNS, CHEESE & BREADCRUMBS

Serves 4

Lemon sole is a very versatile fish to cook. It can be served very simply with a herb sauce or cooked with pretty additional ingredients, as in this case.

INGREDIENTS

4 lemon sole fillets

4 tbsp breadcrumbs (Panko are very good)

3 tbsp cooked peeled prawns

1 tbsp parsley, finely chopped

2 tbsp Parmesan cheese, grated

2 tbsp lemon juice

olive oil

1 lemon, cut into wedges

1 tbsp chives, chopped

Heat the oven to 200°C/390°F/gas mark 6. Place the fillets in an oiled ovenproof dish. In a separate bowl, mix together the breadcrumbs, prawns, parsley and Parmesan. Add as much lemon juice as you need to make the mixture softer before spooning it over the fillets. Sprinkle with some olive oil and the remainder of the lemon juice.

Bake in the oven for 10 minutes or until the topping is golden and smelling wonderful. Serve with wedges of lemon and a sprinkling of chopped chives.

MEGRIM SOLE
WITH CLOTTED CREAM & CHIVES

Serves 4

Megrim sole is a fish which is caught a great deal in the West Country and is as delicious as lemon sole. Sadly, it remains unappreciated by many and much of it is exported.

INGREDIENTS

4 megrim sole, filleted

110g clotted cream

2 tbsp chives, chopped

25g butter

Cornish sea salt and ground black pepper, to taste

¼ tsp paprika

Butter an ovenproof dish that will hold all 4 fish in one layer. Spread the clotted cream and the chives between the fillets of each fish. Dot the top of the fish with a little butter and the salt and pepper to taste.

Bake in a hot oven 230°C/450°F/gas mark 8 for 10 minutes. Dust with paprika to decorate, and serve.

Spinach and new potatoes go well with the megrim.

TORBAY SOLE
STUFFED WITH CRAB & PRAWNS

Serves 4

Torbay sole is lovely and yet is often shunned, simply because it is less well known — in fact its name has been changed from witch sole in an effort to make it more popular. It tastes every bit as good as lemon sole and can be fatter with denser flesh.

INGREDIENTS

4 small or 2 large Torbay soles, filleted

20 prawns

225g mixed crabmeat

225ml double cream

juice of 2 lemons

2 tbsp chives, chopped

Cornish sea salt and ground black pepper, to taste

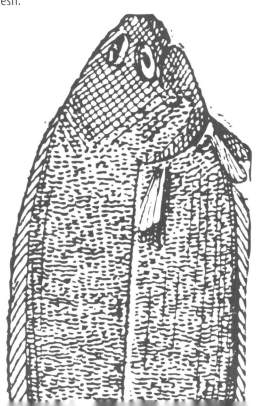

Cut the prawns in half and mix with the crabmeat, most of the chives and the double cream – this is the stuffing mixture. Pour a little of the lemon juice into an ovenproof dish. If the fillets are small, first lay down the bottom fillet, placing some stuffing on top and then covering with the other fillet. If they are large soles, the fillets will need to be cut lengthways, before stuffing them in the same manner.

Add sea salt and ground black pepper to taste and cover with the remainder of the lemon juice – you will have to use your judgement: if the lemons are large you may not need to use all the juice.

Place in a hot oven 230°C/450°F/gas mark 8 for 15-20 minutes, depending on the thickness of the sole – check after 15 minutes to be on the safe side. Decorate with the remainder of the chives.

PRAWNS WITH PASTA, PEAS & COURGETTES

Serves 4

This is a simple, quick and attractive recipe – from store cupboard items. If you don't have any courgettes simply use more peas.

INGREDIENTS

300g pasta of your choice

100g frozen petits pois

olive oil

2 medium courgettes, finely sliced

2 cloves garlic, sliced and chopped

6 spring onions, chopped

150g frozen prawns, either raw or cooked

pinch of dried chilli flakes

100g Feta cheese

2 tbsp parsley, chopped

grated Parmesan, to taste

Cook the pasta of your choice according to the packet instructions, adding the frozen peas 2 minutes before the pasta is ready. Drain.

Meanwhile, heat some olive oil in a large frying pan over a medium low heat. Cook the courgettes, garlic and spring onions until the courgettes are al dente, then add the prawns – if they are raw, you will need to cook them until they are pink. Add a pinch of the chilli flakes. Combine this mixture with the pasta and peas in a serving dish. Crumble over the Feta cheese, add the chopped parsley and mix. Serve with grated Parmesan to taste.

SQUID WITH GARLIC, CORIANDER & OLIVES

Serves 4

Squid (and octopus) look somewhat scary to prepare but fishmongers are only too willing to do the tricky work for you. It is fished all the year but is best in winter. While it is much more popular than it used to be, much of the catch is still exported. This is a very quick and simple dish which has a flavour full of the sunny south.

INGREDIENTS

350g squid, sliced

1 medium onion, finely chopped

2 cloves garlic, chopped

2 tbsp coriander, chopped

12 green olives, pitted and roughly chopped

2 tbsp sherry or white wine

olive oil

1 tbsp pine nuts (optional)

Put a little olive oil in a frying pan and add the onion and garlic, cooking until soft. Add the squid and fry quickly for 2 minutes over a hot flame, turning constantly. Add the olives and the coriander and white wine. Mix together over the heat and serve straight away with plain boiled rice decorated with 1 tablespoon of pine nuts.

HOT SQUID SALAD

Serves 4

Hot salads are always fun to make; they are instant food with the delight of hot ingredients and dressing.

INGREDIENTS

350g squid, roughly sliced

4 spring onions, thinly sliced

225g tomatoes, cut into chunks

10cm piece of cucumber, cut into chunks

1 cabbage lettuce or assorted salad leaves

12 black olives, pitted

2 tbsp assorted herbs, chopped

12 seedless grapes, cut in half

4 tbsp olive oil

1 tbsp white wine vinegar

Cornish sea salt and ground black pepper, to taste

Firstly assemble the salad in a large bowl. Place some of the olive oil in a frying pan and over a high heat, fry the squid for 2 minutes. Add the rest of the olive oil and warm it through, then add the wine vinegar – be careful: it will hiss and steam and make your eyes water!

Pour the squid and dressing over the salad, add salt and ground black pepper to taste. Toss the salad thoroughly until the lettuce begins to wilt and all the ingredients are mixed together. Serve immediately with warm French bread.

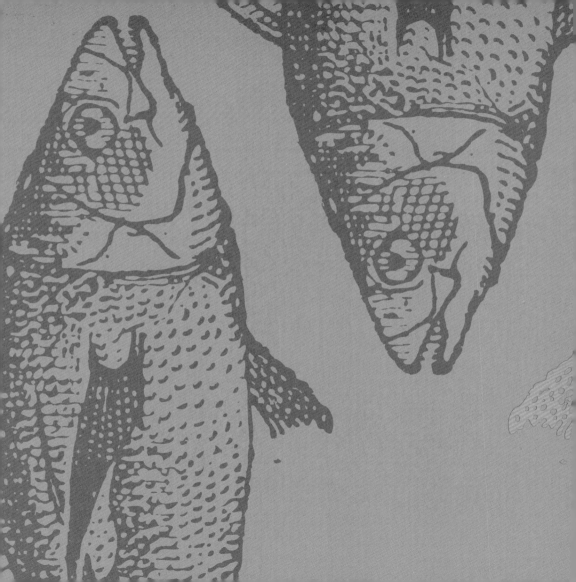

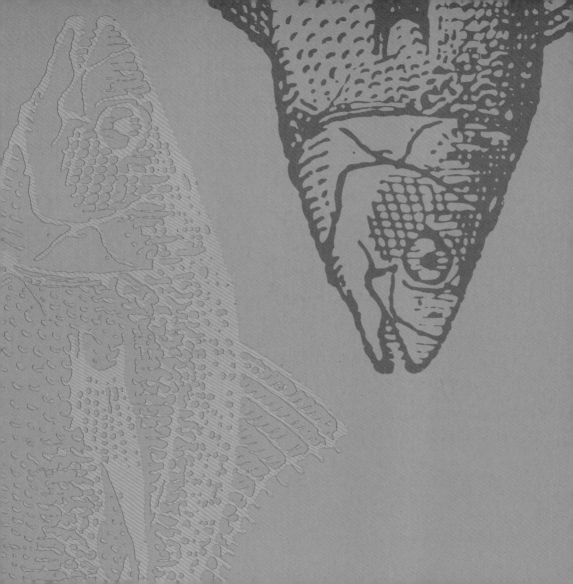

TUNA WITH CORIANDER, LEMON & WHITE WINE

Serves 4

Tuna is caught 3-4 weeks a year out of Newlyn but is always readily available on supermarket fish stalls. Although expensive, tuna is very filling, so the portions can be quite small. It is straightforward to cook and versatile – it looks like pale meat and can be treated very like fillet steak. It is important not to overcook it.

INGREDIENTS

300g tuna, no more than 12mm thick

juice of 1 lemon

½ glass white wine

olive oil

2 tbsp coriander, chopped

2 cloves garlic, chopped

1 medium courgette, roughly chopped, for serving

new potatoes, for serving

Slice the tuna into 4, each weighing 75g. Cover the base of an ovenproof dish with a little olive oil, place the tuna slices in the dish and cover with the rest of the ingredients.

Bake in a hot oven 230°C/450°F/gas mark 8 for 10-15 minutes and serve with new potatoes and courgettes.

TUNA STEW

Serves 4

This is a reminder of holidays in sunnier climates — tuna is readily available in Spain, Portugal and Southern France and because of its meat-like qualities, lends itself to being stewed with Mediterranean vegetables. The French parsley is used here because of the hint of celery in the chopped stalks.

INGREDIENTS

350g tuna, cut into large chunks

1 medium onion, roughly chopped

½ red pepper, roughly chopped

½ green pepper, roughly chopped

1 medium courgette, roughly chopped

1 400g tin chopped tomatoes

2 tsp tomato purée

¼ tsp dried oregano

olive oil

Cornish sea salt and ground black pepper, to taste

1 tbsp French parsley, chopped

plain boiled rice or couscous, for serving

Fry all the vegetables in a little olive oil in an ovenproof casserole over a medium heat. When they are beginning to soften add the tomato purée, tinned tomatoes, oregano, salt and pepper to taste, and lastly the tuna. Mix gently together and place in a medium oven 180°C/350°F/gas mark 4 for about 30 minutes or until the vegetables and tuna are cooked through. Sprinkle the chopped parsley on top and serve with plain boiled rice or couscous.

NOTES

NOTES